Blankinship
Ontario, Oregon
1988

Blankinship
Ontario, Oregon
1988

GAME BIRDS

GAME BIRDS

Illustrated by Maurice Pledger

Written by Charles Coles

CRESCENT BOOKS
New York

This 1988 edition published by Crescent Books,
distributed by Crown Publishers, Inc., 225 Park
Avenue South, New York, New York 10003.

© Copyright Dragon's World Ltd 1983
© Copyright illustrations Maurice John Pledger 1981
© Copyright text Dragon's World Ltd 1983

Originally published in Great Britain by
William Collins Sons & Co Ltd

Library of Congress Cataloging-in-Publication Data
Pledger, Maurice.
    Game birds.

    Reprint. Originally published: Limpsfield, Surrey,
England : Dragon's World, 1983.
    1. Galliformes——Pictorial works.   2. Game and game-
birds——Pictorial works.   3. Birds——Pictorial works.
I. Coles, Charles, 1917-   . II. Title.
QL696.G2P55   1987   598'.61'00222   87-20179
ISBN 0-517-65517-9

Printed and bound in Spain by
Edime/Atanes Láinez - Graphiberia
D. L.: M. 42.195-1987

For Pietra and Douglas

Acknowledgements

A great number of people – too numerous to mention – have assisted me in the production of this book, but in particular I would like to list a few names for special mention.

G. Ray Arnett, *Assistant Secretary, Fish, Wildlife and Parks, Department of the Interior, Washington, D.C.*

E. V. Komarek, *Tall Timbers Research Station, Tallahassee, Florida, U.S.A.*

Dr Vidar Marcstrom, *Institute of Zoophysiology, Uppsala, Sweden.*

Professor Robert J. Robel, *Kansas State University.*

Bo Thelander, *Swedish Hunters Association, Stockholm.*

Also members of the research staff of the Game Conservancy:

G. R. Potts, BSc., PhD., M. Street, MSc., MIBiol., G. J. M. Hirons, BSc., DPhil. and R. E. Green, BSc., PhD.

Our thanks are also due to Michael R. Long, A.S.I.A.D. – the designer of this book, and Linden Artists for their helpful co-ordination.

Finally I would also like to record my appreciation of the very professional assistance given me by my secretary Miss Wendy Smith of the Game Conservancy.

Contents

List of Plates   *Page 11*
Foreword: *H.R.H. The Prince Philip,*
              Duke of Edinburgh K.G., K.T.   *13*
Introduction to the Artist: *C. H. Freeman*   *15*
Game Conservation: *Charles Coles*   *17*
Pheasant: *Phasianus colchicus*   *20*
Reeves's Pheasant: *Syrmaticus reevesi*   *24*
Quail: *Coturnix coturnix*   *28*
California Quail: *Lophortyx californicus*   *32*
Bobwhite Quail: *Colinus virginianus*   *36*
Grey Partridge: *Perdix perdix*   *40*
Red-legged Partridge: *Alectoris rufa*   *44*
Capercaillie: *Tetrao urogallus*   *48*
Black Grouse: *Lyrurus tetrix*   *52*
Red Grouse: *Lagopus lagopus scoticus*   *56*
Hazel Hen: *Tetrastes bonasia*   *60*
Ptarmigan: *Lagopus mutus*   *64*
Willow Grouse: *Lagopus lagopus*   *68*
Ruffed Grouse: *Bonasa umbellus*   *72*
Sage Grouse: *Centrocercus urophasianus*   *76*
Greater Prairie Chicken: *Tympanuchus cupido*   *80*
Wild Turkey: *Meleagris galloparvo sp.*   *84*
Great Bustard: *Otis tarda*   *88*
Mallard: *Anas platyrhynchos*   *92*
Teal: *Anas crecca*   *96*
Wigeon: *Anas penelope*   *100*
Canada Goose: *Branta canadensis*   *104*
Woodcock: *Scolopax rusticola*   *108*
Common Snipe and Jack Snipe: *112*
Capella gallinago / Lymnocryptes minimus
Epilogue   *115*
Select Bibliography   *117*

List of Plates

I   Wild Ring-necked Pheasant calling

II   Reeves's Pheasants

III   Pair of Common Quail with nest and eggs

IV   Pair of California Quail

V   Pair of Bobwhite Quail on maize stalk

VI   Pair of Grey Partridges – Male in flight

VII   Red-legged Partridges – young bird dusting

VIII   Capercaillie on pine branch – Male

IX   Blackcock displaying

X   Red Grouse becking

XI   Pair of Hazel Grouse on woodland floor

XII   Ptarmigan in winter plumage

XIII   Willow Grouse in Autumn plumage

XIV   Ruffed Grouse in Autumn woods

XV   Pair of Sage Grouse – Male displaying

XVI   Prairie Chicken on booming ground – Male

XVII   Wild Turkey displaying in woodland

XVIII   Great Bustard – female on nest

XIX   Mallard Drake by the water's edge

XX   Cock Teal by reeds and wild mint

XXI   Cock Wigeon in reeds at water's edge

XXII   Canada Goose and goslings at nest

XXIII   Woodcock with nest and eggs

XXIV   Common Snipe wading –
            Jack Snipe on edge of marsh

Foreword
by

His Royal Highness
The Prince Philip
Duke of Edinburgh *K.G., K.T.*

BUCKINGHAM PALACE.

Linnaeus devised a wonderful system for the classification of animals and plants, but for the less scientific, I suspect that animals come in four groups - wild, domestic, game, and of course, pest. The descriptions convey the human relationship to each group and in the case of wild, domestic and pest it is fairly straightforward. Game, however, is a different matter altogether and the text of this book written by Charles Coles, Director of the Game Conservancy, explains that difference as far as game birds are concerned and a great deal of other information besides. There may be anomalies and contradictions in the simultaneous conservation and exploitation of game birds yet, paradoxically therein lies their security.

The marvellous illustrations by Maurice Pledger are in the very best tradition of bird paintings and for those, like myself, with an interest in game birds and a weakness for such pictures the book will give endless pleasure.

1981

Introduction to the Artist

I first became acquainted with the paintings of Maurice Pledger when I happened to pass a gallery which had one of his pictures in the window, and was drawn inside to enquire of the artist and his work. Since then it has been my great pleasure to know him personally and follow his career.

His early work showed great artistic merit and led me to believe that we had a successor to the great Archibald Thorburn, who, like Maurice Pledger, matured early in his career and was considered the best painter of birds and wildlife when he was thirty.

With maturity Maurice has acquired the ability to bring his subjects to life and to paint them in the round. His birds have that natural brightness of eye, freshness of colour, and attention to detail which reflects his love and feeling for the subject and his knowledge as a naturalist.

The compositions are arranged in such a manner as to focus the attention on the subject itself with no background distractions. His pictures are a work of art in the full visual sense, and are not dissimilar in style to the work of the great Victorian ornithological artist, John Gould.

Maurice enjoys his work and his humility to his talent is so refreshing and his success well deserved.

C. H. Freeman

Game Conservation

E VER since early man daubed or scratched simple pictures of the animals he hunted on the walls of his cave dwellings, the Chase – with its own laws and traditions – has continued to play a part of some significance in the lives of a large number of people. Throughout the ages the hunt and its quarry have always been an inspiration for painters, wood carvers, sculptors: even poets and musicians. This was more than just a legacy inherited from the prehistoric days before man turned from hunting to husbandry and more pastoral occupations. As civilisations developed, the intrinsic importance of acquiring the meat, bones and skins that were vital to life itself naturally diminished. But the challenge and excitement of hunting wild creatures, often in beautiful and remote surroundings, has remained.

Words cannot properly describe the emotions of a wildfowler waiting in the half dark for the sound of wings approaching from seawards, with a background of marsh noises – strange and not always identifiable – water running, mud oozing, a distant ship's engine. Nor can they reflect the feelings of a roe deer stalker on a spring morning in the beech woods – the sun low and the young leaves still a translucent green. Here there are different smells from those on the foreshore – mosses, earth, bark: the rank bitterness of nettles, old ivy and elder, mixed with the sweetness of wild flowers.

An American game biologist, Professor Aldo Leopold, described his personal feelings about the extra dimension given to a landscape by the presence of wild game. Of their beautiful upland gamebird, the ruffed grouse, he said: "Everybody knows that the autumn landscape in the north woods is the land, plus a red maple, plus a ruffed grouse. In terms of conventional physics, the grouse represent only a millionth of either the mass or the energy of an acre. Yet subtract the grouse and the whole thing is dead."

The absence or presence of red grouse has the same effect on people who know and understand our own heather covered moors.

As shooting became more popular it was perhaps inevitable that some of the participants would indulge in excesses resulting in the decline of certain quarry species. The added pressures of intensive agriculture and the alarming destruction of wildlife habitat probably provided the final jolt that was needed to show farmers and sportsmen that game should be cared for and husbanded like a crop: that only the surplus created by good management should be harvested, and careful thought given to the seasons to come.

In many countries these lessons have now been learned and the shooting man is in the forefront of the conservation movement. On a well managed sporting property there are always more song-birds, wild flowers, butterflies and other forms of wildlife than on land where there is no interest in shooting and game conservation.

For generations the hunter has left his imprint on the landscape in the form of an attractive and varied countryside designed to provide the best possible conditions for his quarry. The mixed woodland that is planted as a pheasant covert encourages many more species of wildlife that the dark blanket of spruce designed solely for timber output. On land where no thought is given to habitat protection, instead of farms with sheltering hedgerows and a reasonable interspersion of other forms of cover, there are only bleak horizons of monoculture. Incidentally hedges, as well as affording valuable nesting and escape cover, can also provide reservoirs of useful predatory insects that control cereal pests.

We owe a great debt to our ancestors who shot, hunted and fished, for they created the warm, intimate countryside that is now at risk from the combination of agrochemicals, machines, drainage schemes, commercial afforestation, and other forms of land use, which are not always as sympathetic to wildlife as they could afford to be. In Great Britain, nevertheless, we are more fortunate than in many countries. If the traveller drives through parts of Central Europe today – through mile after mile of maize, uniform grass prairies, or even extensive vineyards, unrelieved by a spinney, an overgrown pit, or a smallholder's plot of cabbages and potatoes – he will observe that the partridges that once thrived in profusion have almost disappeared; that the hares are rapidly declining; that the wild pheasant has had to be replaced by the reared bird, and that the Great Bustard is restricted to only a few sanctuary areas. If, when the revolutionary State and collective farming enterprises were being planned in the 1950's, a single countryman who loved his partridges had been present at the discussion table, the landscape could still be attractive today, the wildlife would have suffered less, and there would have been very little difference in the crop yield.

We can no longer afford too many poppies in the corn, nor fields of ten acres, nor unkempt hedges twenty feet wide. Furthermore, partridges and pheasants do not need them. With a few compromises we can increase our game and wildlife populations and retain the beautiful countryside that we inherited from those generations that really cared about such things.

Charles Coles

PHEASANT

Phasianus colchicus

Plate I

THE pheasant has been with us for a long time.

The oldest fossilised remains of pheasants, which were recently discovered in China, go back 20 million years. Other fossils of *phasianidae* from the Miocene period have been identified in France, so it seems likely that pheasants occurred in great Britain at the same time. Nobody knows exactly when they became extinct in Europe.

The re-introduction of the pheasant to England was carried out by the Romans: for some time it had been a part of their villa life, kept like the peacock to eat as well as to admire. Besides the species we now call the English Black-neck (*Phasianus colchicus*) it is possible that they also introduced one of the ring-necked breeds such as the Chinese (*Phasianus torquatus*), as a mosaic has recently been found in a Roman villa in Gloucestershire, depicting a pheasant with a clear white ring round its neck.

The Black-neck pheasant was recorded by classical Greek writers as originally living along the banks of the river Phasis in a land bordering the Black Sea then called Colchis. Hence the scientific name *Phasianus colchicus*. The region was described as consisting mostly of the slow-flowing river and its shallow slimey waters, fringed with marshes and forests. The Phasis is now called the river Rioni which is in the Soviet State of Georgia.

After the Roman importations many other species were subsequently introduced into the British Isles. The pheasant is now a common bird almost everywhere. Its family is a large one comprising nearly 50 species; 32 are classed as True pheasants, but of these only half a dozen or so are likely to be recognised individually by the average game shot. Most of the pheasants that hatch out in the wild are ring-necked hybrids: a mixture of the many varieties that have been released from time to time by landowners trying to re-stock their coverts with new breeds that they thought might fly faster, look prettier or taste better.

The common pheasant favours the edge of woodlands, preferably consisting of mixed species and mixed age groups. It is also found on suitable farmlands and in areas of marsh or reedland. In spite of being able to fly very strongly it prefers to walk and will roost on the ground if there are no trees in the vicinity.

It eats an extremely wide variety of animal and vegetable foods – wheat being its favourite cereal. In addition to the fruits, seeds and leaves of wild plants and trees, some roots and tubers are consumed, also many insects and their larvae. I have observed them picking over seaweed on a Scottish tideline, and gobbling up tiny frogs in a Danube marsh. Their tastes are catholic.

The breeding season begins about mid-February when the cocks start to show signs of aggression and spar amongst themselves. During March and the first half of April, the dominant cocks establish breeding territories of approximately 4–5 acres: this is accompanied by crowing. Cocks without territories do not crow. The hens tend to wander about in small groups at this time, mating indiscriminately with different cocks. When egg-laying starts, they settle down on individual home ranges, which can overlap the territories of several cocks. There is no pair bond.

Egg-laying extends from mid-March to early June, with a peak in late April. The nests are made in a variety of cover situations, such as brambles or nettles a little way inside a wood, in scrubland, a hedgerow, or a farm crop in which situation they are often destroyed by machinery. the average clutch consists of about 12 olive-coloured eggs which are incubated for 23–24 days by the hen alone. Foxes, stoats and the crow family are the main predators. Should a nest be destroyed a hen will almost invariably attempt to re-nest after about 10 days.

Most chicks hatch between the 18th and 30th May: the usual brood being about 10. A plentiful supply of insects and good weather greatly assist chick survival. If a hen loses her brood at a very early age she will occasionally re-lay.

The crowing of a cock pheasant is difficult to describe in print: it usually consists of a two-note utterance "Karrr̃k-Karrr̃k", but there are many variants.

They will crow noisily before going up to roost: this is called "cocking", and they will also drum loudly with their wings like a barnyard rooster.

The flesh of the hen pheasant is more succulent than that of the cock. A hen weighs about $2\frac{1}{2}$ lb and a cock $3\frac{3}{4}$ lb, though much heavier birds are sometimes recorded.

Wild Ring-necked Pheasant calling

REEVES'S PHEASANT

Syrmaticus reevesi

Plate II

MANY species of pheasant were known to have existed in China in antiquity. An ancient Chinese character which represents "pheasant" was certainly used during the Shang or Yin Dynasty: the accepted date for the end of this dynasty being 1027 B.C. Much later, about a thousand years ago during the T'ang Dynasty, there were specific references to the Reeves pheasant. Its barred tail feathers, sometimes over six feet in length, were used in Court ceremonies as standards, fans and hat adornments.

This striking pheasant came from Northern and Central China – living in the higher, tree covered hills up to 6,000 feet. Marco Polo, the Venetian traveller who spent seventeen years in Cathay, was familiar with the species. After his return in 1298 he noted – in the language of a contemporary translator – "There be plenty of Feysants and very greate, for one of them is as big as two of ours, with tayles of eight, nine and ten spannes long." The naturalist Temminck later gave it the name *veneratus*, at the time believing that the Chinese venerated the bird and had superstitious ideas about it: the French still call it the *faisan vénéré*.

After Marco Polo's description of it not much more was heard of this pheasant until 1808, when a Mr Beale was reported to be keeping some specimens in his aviary in Macao. The original cock pheasant in the collection lived for thirteen years. It was not until 1831 that the first specimens from the Beale aviary were brought to England by a Mr Reeves, and then thirty years were to pass before they were successfully bred in captivity. Not long afterwards sporting estate owners began to release them into the wild. They proved to be a hardy breed, magnificent fliers and – according to all who have eaten them – they are by far the most delicious.

Sir J. G. Millais shot them as they came over in company with common pheasants and blackcock "amongst the wildest and shaggiest of Scotch scenery in a country which must to a great extent resemble the true home of the bird in question", and described how the "long-tailed sky-rockets left the others behind and came forward at a pace which was little short of terrific."

Since then many sportsmen have commented on their speed, and also on their ability to brake very suddenly when travelling at full speed. As a breed they tend to be quarrelsome and to drive away the more ordinary sporting pheasants, though they will also hybridise with them – only the male crosses being fertile.

When attemps were made to acclimatise them in unsuitable surroundings – as frequently happened in the early experimental days – they would take wing and travel up to thirty miles at a stretch, so they never really became popular as a covert pheasant. Some years ago a large-scale re-stocking experiment took place in central France, which confirmed that they would not settle in the typical, mixed woodlands to be found on many an arable farm. After only a few years and seemingly adequate measures for their conservation most of them had disappeared.

They are really pheasants of the forest.

Reeves's Pheasants

QUAIL

Coturnix coturnix

Plate III

THE quail, which is the smallest of our gamebirds, looks rather like a miniature partridge. It is the only British gamebird that migrates. From bill to tail it measures no more than 7 ins, whereas a cock partridge is a little over 12 ins, and it weighs 3–4 oz. Its ventriloquial call, which is supposed to resemble "*wet-my-lips*", will carry a long way on a summer's evening.

The quail is a bird of rather secretive habits, and except on migration does not take wing easily unless threatened, preferring to move about quietly in cornfields, rough grasses, clover and any other such vegetation which affords concealment. When it does fly it rises quickly and churrs away for a relatively short distance before dropping down again. Quail are now fully protected in the United Kingdom and may no longer be shot, but when shooting was allowed a dog was almost essential to get them to flush.

Though quail are widely distributed in Europe, North Africa and Western Asia, the numbers in the United Kingdom fluctuate greatly, and one speaks of "quail years". These occur to some extent because we are on the edge of their summer migration range, and the effect of the weather on this movement can be considerable. The birds usually arrive in May and most depart again in October, migrating almost exclusively at night. A large influx of quail seems to coincide with particularly warm, dry spring weather in France, and south-east winds which help the quail to overshoot their normal European breeding grounds.

Groups of quail are termed "bevies".

The nest is usually made in growing corn, the clutch varying from 7–12. The colour of the eggs consists of a background of cream or pale tea, speckled or blotched with various shades of brown. When, a little while after the arrival of the males, the hens settle in to their breeding areas, their primary concern seems to be to find a suitable nest site rather than look around for a mate. When this first object has been achieved they start responding to the overtures of any singing cocks that have meantime secured a nearby territory. Although the cock is attentive during incubation and the pair sing duets, only the hen sits on the eggs and normally only the female parent looks after the brood when hatched.

Being small and rather elusive, quail have not been studied in the same detail as partridges, but it is assumed that they eat much the same food. They have been observed taking ground-dwelling insects and their larvae, as well as plant foods such as cereals, and the fallen seeds of chickweeds, fat-hen, dock, vetches, *polygonums* and the like. Occasionally they will feed on large insects such as locusts or praying mantises.

In some of the Mediterranean countries migrating quail were at one time netted for the table in hundreds of thousands – not only in the autumn but also in the spring just before the breeding season. Many an impecunious midshipman or subaltern serving in the Middle East – innocent of the implications of wildlife – will remember quail-and-rice as one of the cheapest dishes on a restaurant menu. Like trout in a tank the live quail awaited their fate in wicker baskets on the pavement or terrace.

The practice of netting the migrants has now been reduced by international agreement; quail served in British restaurants are the Japanese species which are reared in captivity like poultry.

Pair of Common Quail with nest and eggs

M.J.PLEDGER

CALIFORNIA QUAIL

Lophortyx californicus

Plate IV

"THE brush country and the plains are covered with little crested gray partridges, which like those of Europe live gregariously, but in coveys of three or four hundred. They are fat and of good flavour."

This was the first mention of the California quail by a French traveller, Jean Francois Galaup de la Pérouse, who visited Monterey in 1786. A few years later Archibald Menzies, a British naturalist and surgeon on a round-the-world voyage in the "Discovery", described it as being "of a dark lead colour, beautifully speckled with black, white and ferruginous colours with a crest of reverted black feathers on the crown of its head." He also commented on the delicacy of its flavour.

The California quail is certainly a charming, handsome little bird – weighing 6 to 7 oz – with a perky behaviour and melodious calls. The hen, which is less strikingly marked, has a much smaller and less showy topknot. The species is distributed for about two thousand miles along the west coast from the British Columbia border in the north right down to the southern tip of the state.

Soon after the colonists arrived, the quail started to increase as a result of the pioneer work on the land which progressively offered a more attractive environment in their traditional habitats, and also extended their range to new frontiers. Clearings were opened up in the forests, hedges made their appearance in the prairies, grain was grown in new areas and exotic annual plants including filarees – or storksbills – legumes and their attendant weeds, came into the country from Europe and helped provide more quail food. Many more water areas were developed – vital in the summer months when temperatures are high and the young birds are being reared. Quail tend to increase in years of good rainfall and decrease when it is dry. In rainy years the forbs grow better and produce heavier crops of the seeds enjoyed by the quail.

The steady improvement in quail numbers continued until the 1890's, but eventually with the marketing of hundreds of thousands of birds for cheap food at around 10 cents apiece, a decline set in. In 1901 the authorities prohibited their sale and introduced a bag limit for the hunters. By the turn of the century a more efficient agriculture was also beginning to have its effect: the mosaic patterns that suited quails and partridges were dissolving into block farming, and reducing both food and cover.

Professor Aldo Leopold, that great student of game, said nearly half a century ago: "Game can be restored by the creative use of the same tools which have heretofor destroyed it – axe, plough, cow, fire and gun. A favourable alignment of these forces sometimes came about in pioneer days by accident." It is still the maxim of today's game managers.

As to the social life of California quail, the winter coveys or flocks may number from 25 to many hundreds. At night – unlike the Bobwhite – the birds will roost in dense trees or shrubs out of reach of their enemies. Roosting cover is an important component in their habitat requirements.

In the early spring the coveys disperse and pairing commences: with unpaired males frequently establishing crowing territories in the vicinity of mated pairs. The species is virtually monogamous and the cock an attentive mate and parent; if the hen is killed he will sometimes take over incubation duties. The nests, which are often near water, tend to be extremely well hidden in grassy, weedy cover. The hens are secretive about giving their presence away when approaching or leaving. The cock is always watchful, perching on a nearby vantage point so that he can see all round. He will also remain on guard when the hen is off feeding and when the young are foraging. During this period his own food intake becomes somewhat irregular and he loses weight.

Casualties from predation are high and re-nesting normal. More unusual is the practice, not perhaps fully studied, of the cock taking over the brood when they are about two weeks of age, leaving the hen to mate with another cock and raise a separate brood.

The quail's diet varies according to what is available, but seeds and leafy greenstuff, particularly sprouting legumes, are the main ingredients; also fruit, berries, acorns and cereals, including rice. The forbs that are popular with quail are also among the favourite foods of farm livestock, and in this competition the quail is the loser. Planned grazing can help.

The first call of a California quail, heard by me in a Nevada suburb, was unexpected. Across a smokey room full of cocktail people, and through and beyond some French windows, came a clear *cow* call on a late afternoon. Eventually I traced the source: a beautiful cock quail, sitting on a bird table and behaving – uncharacteristically I thought – like a domestic Surrey blackbird. But I was wrong, for they are evidently quite sociable and frequent backyards and bird baths.

Pair of California Quail

BOBWHITE QUAIL

Colinus virginianus

Plate V

THE bobwhite – one of several species of quail – is probably the most popular upland gamebird in North America. It is mainly a bird of the Eastern and Southern States, from the Dakotas in the north down to the Texas-Mexico border and beyond; but there are also isolated pockets where stock has been introduced.

It is a most attractive, plump little gamebird, weighing about 6 oz. There are a number of differences between the sexes, but the most easily recognised is the white throat and chin of the male, which in the female is buff coloured. It inhabits fairly open country interspersed with brushy cover or scattered woodlands. Grasslands are used particularly in the spring for nesting: in the summer and fall bobwhites prefer arable farming land which provides more food, loafing, roosting and dusting sites. In winter, scrub country and tree plantations come into their own, providing extra shelter and escape cover. Water or adequate moisture is a requirement for good densities of bobwhite, which in attractive farming areas can reach about a pair to four acres, or one bird per acre just before the hunting season.

As with partridges, the social unit in winter is the covey; this tends to be fairly sedentary and occupies a range of 50 acres or a good deal less, depending on the availability of good food and cover. The coveys which form up after the "fall shuffle" appear to have no particular family, age or sex composition. Each group consists of about 10 birds or more, which seems to be about the right number required to maintain the necessary temperature when roosting. This they do by bunching together to form a tightly packed circle, all the birds facing outwards.

The food of bobwhites varies according to the locality, but once past the insect-eating chick stage, they will take the seeds of legumes, a variety of herbaceous weeds, maize and other cereals. Acorns can be an important item of diet in the fall.

Quail lay about the same number of eggs as grey partridges and their incubation period is also identical. The nests are usually built in light herbaceous cover and often concealed by having some of the adjacent vegetation bent inwards over the top to form a roof. In spite of this, nesting casualties are often heavy – up to 60 or 70 per cent. Such losses are to some extent counteracted by the hens re-nesting, sometimes two or three times. The life expectancy of the bobwhite is short – usually less than one year – so few birds survive to breed more than once. The clear, three-note call or whistle of the bobwhite has been described as *ah-bob-white* or *bob-bob-white*, thereby providing this quail with its name. Peak calling occurs in June at hatching time, and is undertaken by unmated as well as mated males.

As with other quarry species conservation of the correct habitat is the first essential of quail management. In Georgia, I was able to observe this being effectively and economically carried out using fire as a management tool, in much the same way as on a grouse moor. The art of controlled burning to improve wildlife range was never better demonstrated than on the hunting estates I visited. To see the vegetation rapidly greening up out of blackened shrubs and tree trunks in a chessboard pattern and providing perfect quail cover was of great interest.

Here, on some Georgia estates, bobwhites were hunted over dogs with artistry and ceremonial. Coachmen in livery took the guns and pointers in open carriages to the different beats. Although the bobwhite prefers to walk or run away from danger, when a covey does flush it explodes into the air and then usually scatters in all directions. To find these distant birds there were additional teams of pointers handled by outriders on quarter horses. Only a certain number of birds per covey were allowed to be hunted.

In spite of dedicated research and careful shooting, in most areas the bobwhite continues to decline due to a gradual deterioration of its habitat, and the increased scarcity of food that follows in the wake of intensive agriculture.

From time to time since the nineteenth-century bobwhites have been introduced into England, but sooner or later the liberated birds have died out. One little colony from a 1964 release is, however, thought to be still surviving in the Scilly Islands.

Pair of Bobwhite Quail on maize stalk

GREY PARTRIDGE

Perdix perdix

Plate VI

THE plumage of the grey partridge is commonplace rather than spectacular, and its voice is not unlike a key turning in a rusty lock: yet it has always held the affection of English sportsmen more than any other quarry. It is probably the first gamebird to which a young shot is introduced towards the end of the summer holidays: the first retrieve allowed to a young gundog under training. It vies with the red grouse as the finest bird to shoot, and with the woodcock as the most delicious to eat.

There are two species of partridge in this country: the native, common or grey partridge and the introduced redlegged or Frenchman which is described elsewhere. In rapid flight or if seen some distance away, the inexperienced observer may not be able to distinguish easily between the two species, but at close range there can be no confusion.

Up until the late thirties the grey partridge was the shooting man's main quarry: the sales of cartridges rose and fell annually according to the success or otherwise of the wild partridge's breeding season. In those days the vagaries of the weather during Ascot week were the main factors to influence the survival of the chicks. Nowadays, although the weather still has a major effect on their fate, the many pressures of intensive farming, the erosion of hedgerows and other vital cover, the rain of pesticides that are too often used unselectively, the burning of stubbles and so on, have all contributed extra dimensions to the problem.

Scientists of the Game Conservancy have always given priority to studying the partridge. It is an indicator species, a barometer of the welfare of so many other forms of wildlife that live on arable farms. In fact, the partridge probably holds the key to how we can achieve an acceptable compromise between food production, wildlife survival and the preservation of the warm, intimate landscape that is so much more attractive than the bleak alternative of a hedgeless monoculture.

Partridges spend the autumn and winter in family groups or coveys, which break up during the first few warm days of early spring. When pairing takes place there is no inbreeding within a covey: the young cocks mate with females from outside coveys. Where an old pair have both survived the winter the two will remate. The partridge is monogamous.

The well-hidden nests are usually made in hedgerows, rough clumps of cover such as nettles, brambles and overgrown grasses; or in silage and hay crops, in which case they are all too often destroyed by the machines at cutting time. About 15 olive coloured eggs constitute the normal clutch, and the peak hatch occurs around June 15th. Both cock and hen take part in brooding the chicks. Farm machines and predators take a heavy toll of nests, sitting hens and young. Depending on the weather, half to three-quarters of the chicks will perish: starvation due to lack of vital insects to eat being the main cause. If there is sufficient food available, the tiny chicks, which during their first few days of life look not unlike large bumblebees, can fill their crops quickly and get back under the parent to be sheltered from inclement weather. But if the insects or their food plants have been destroyed, the baby partridges will have to spend a long and exhausting time searching for food; in a bad season exposed to the cold and wet, and always an easy target for predators.

Once past the chick stage the young partridges eat unripe weed seeds, buds, other plant food, and in due course grain. At night they roost fairly close together on the ground – the action being called jugging or jukking.

On farms and estates where a traditional habitat has been maintained, in a favourable season partridges are capable of a rapid build-up, provided the old fashioned hedgerow-keeping concerned with nest protection and tunnel-trapping is not neglected.

After the guns have gone up in the rack for the last time, most of my own generation of sportsmen will, I think, tend to remember – not a gleaming bronze pheasant soaring above the autumn woods, nor a teal springing up out of a half-lit pool with dripping wings; nor majestic capercaillie, nor piping golden plover. Our memories will surely be of a whirring covey of partridges bursting over a thorn hedge: the surrounding English countryside warm and sweet with October scents.

Pair of Grey Partridges – Male in flight

M J PLEDGER

RED-LEGGED PARTRIDGE

Alectoris rufa

Plate VII

THERE are four *Alectoris* partridge species: the red-legged, the barbary, the rock and the chukar, frequenting a variety of habitats which stretch from the United Kingdom to Northern India. In England red-legs are an introduced species and are sometimes called "French partridges", referring to their country of origin. The first successful introduction took place in Suffolk c.1770, after some failures during the previous century. The original consignment of birds were a present from Louis XIV to Charles II after the latter's return from his exile in Europe, where he became interested in the new sport of shooting birds "on the wing."

Within a relatively short time of their introduction into the Eastern counties the French partridges were successfully breeding in the wild and spreading out quite rapidly. They did not, as was commonly supposed, compete with or displace our native grey partridges, but they were very unpopular with our English sportsmen who customarily shot over pointers and setters. Whereas the grey partridges would obligingly squat in a clump of turnips or the long stubbles until flushed by the dogs, the sneaky foreign birds would creep away unnoticed while the dog was on point – leaving a furious and frustrated sportsman with his prize several hundred yards distant. Gamekeepers often smashed the eggs of red-legs in an attempt to keep their numbers down.

Today, the adaptable red-leg is a welcome quarry even though it does not fly as well in flat country as our own grey partridge. It also presents an easier target, tending to come over in one's and two's rather than bursting into view as a covey. As the most sought after gamebird of Spain, however, it is considered a magnificent flier – crossing mountain ravines out of shot, swirling like grouse over the tops of olive groves, and suddenly standing on its tail in the air when alarmed.

In England these partridges are commonly found on well-drained farmland, particularly where there is a reasonable proportion of arable. They also occur on sandy heaths, chalk downlands and in scrub areas. In the hot countries numbers are highest where the land provides water or moisture in some form, a sufficiency of cereals, and shade from the great heat. Unlike grey partridges, the red-leg hens do not cover their eggs when they leave the nest, and casualties from predation are high. At home their enemies are the same as beset pheasants and our native partridges – the habitual predators that hunt hedgerows and woodland fringes. On the Iberian peninsula the large Montpelier snake, the lizard, *Lacerta lepida*, and wild boar also cause considerable losses.

A clutch of eggs will average 12–14 eggs: the background is pale sand coloured, sparingly marked with reddish flecks. The main hatching takes places in early June.

The red-leg has a curious habit of sometimes laying two clutches – one for the cock to incubate. A pair will thus produce two broods, one for each parent. Between the completion of the first clutch and the bird – normally the cock – going down on these eggs, there is often a lapse of three weeks or more while the second clutch is being laid. In spite of such delays the eggs hatch quite normally. After hatching, the two broods usually go their separate ways. If the cock is not provided with a separate nest, which current research suggests occurs with about 25 per cent of the pairs, he tends to leave his hen soon after she has started incubating and join an all-male group or a mixed group with hens that have lost their nests or broods.

If after hatching suitable food for the chicks is available nearby, the broods are not likely to move far, but if there is insufficient food in the locality the young brood may range up to 300 yards a day. The diet of red-legs is much the same as that of grey partridges, except that the former seem to be able to survive on high protein vegetable foods, if insects are lacking. The weather is an important factor in chick survival.

Red-legs are a little heavier than grey partridges – a good cock weighing 18 oz or more. The sexes are basically similar, but an expert should be able to recognise the chauvinistic posture of the male, particularly when perching masterfully on a rock. Cocks that have hatched off young often adopt a feminine, broody manner. Young birds will have the outer two flight feathers pointed rather than rounded, and in our British strains they will also have a faint cream tip.

According to gourmets, the darker meat of the red-leg has a less delicate flavour than that of the English partridge.

Red-legged Partridges – young bird dusting

CAPERCAILLIE

Tetrao urogallus

Plate VIII

THE capercaillie is the largest of all living British gamebirds, being about the size of a small turkey – the male weighing up to 12 lb. Swedish birds can be much heavier. The cock is a handsome, dark bird, appearing almost black when glimpsed in the tops of pine trees, though at close quarters its plumage will be seen to be made up of dark greys, irridescent greens, and browns flecked with white. In flight a large white area becomes visible, particularly under the wings of the bird.

The hen is smaller, with a background of mottled reddish-brown, barred with darker tones, blending well with the woodland floor of heather and fallen pine needles where she nests.

Caper are also found in Scandinavia in the most northern pine forests in the world, as well as in northern parts of the Soviet Union and elsewhere in Central Europe in areas such as the Alps and the Pyrenees. Their preferred habitat consists of natural pine forest, or mixed pine and broad-leaved woodlands, with glades and clearings where heather and various berried plants, such as bilberry, can be found. In natural forests interspersed with open spaces and with trees of uneven age, there are often numbers of old isolated pines, known in Scotland as "grannies", which are much favoured by caper. Many such trees have horizontal branches which are used for roosting and winter feeding. In commercial forests there is little ground vegetation owing to shading out, and few lateral branches.

In the seventeenth century the "wode-henne" became extinct in England and Wales, and somewhere between 1770 and 1785 – due to the eventual disappearance of the indigenous Caledonian pine forests – it died out in Scotland. The poacher and the hunter probably accelerated their demise. When they disappeared from Ireland is not precisely known.

In 1837, during a period when the Scottish hillsides were being replanted with pines, a successful re-introduction of birds from Sweden took place on a Perthshire estate. Several young were reared in captivity and released, and additional eggs produced from captive stock were placed in greyhen nests – a technique that proved successful.

With regard to the caper's diet, it forages mainly on the ground during the warmer half of the year, and in the trees during the colder half. In the winter and early spring therefore its food is taken mostly from pines and larches. Later in the year bilberry, bracken shoots, heather, cereals and a great variety of other vegetable foods are eaten. These great woodland grouse will sometimes damage seedling trees in forest nurseries, particularly if they are near plantations or mature trees adopted by them, and from time to time foresters have regarded them as pests.

In April, normally in the very early morning, the cocks start displaying at small communal leks both to intimidate other cocks and to captivate the hens. The hens will only mate with a mature, dominant cock – his position in the male hierarchy being measured by the number of days he is present at the lek, the frequency of songs and display activities he performs, the outcome of his fights and so on. It is this time of the year that the curious metallic clicking call is emitted by the cocks. The onset of egg-laying varies according to local conditions, but is usually towards the end of April. The eggs have a pale reddish-buff background, speckled and blotched with darker tones. The clutch averages about six. The nest, lined with pine needles, is usually made at the base of an old conifer, sometimes in the heather on open moorland, and very occasionally in a tree using the old nest structure of the previous occupant. The young can fly at an early age.

In some countries the capercaillie is regarded as a big game trophy and shot with a small bore rifle. In the Balkans this stalking takes place during the spring when the cocks lose some of their wariness whilst engaged in their courtship display. In Scandinavia they are sometimes stalked at dawn when calling from the tree tops during the winter months. Elsewhere in Europe the males are shot on their display grounds. One would think that this cannot be a biologically sound practice, for birds that have gained a place on the lek must be the strongest genetic stock. In Scotland it is usual to drive capercaillie over the valleys; owing to their speed and the height at which they often fly they can be very difficult to hit.

Compared to the production of young by other members of the grouse family the capercaillie figure is low. Whereas 30 per cent to 50 per cent of a red grouse population can normally be harvested, the annual bag of caper is restricted to about 15 per cent.

The meat is something of an acquired taste, for as a result of the pine needles in the diet there are often undertones of turpentine in the flesh.

Capercaillie on pine branch – Male

M.J.PLEDGER.

BLACK GROUSE

Lyrurus tetrix

Plate IX

THE male is called a blackcock, the female a greyhen: together they are referred to as blackgame. The cock, with its lyre-shaped tail, white wing bar, and glossy purplish-black plumage is easy to recognise. His scarlet wattle is also characteristic. The cryptically coloured hen could possibly be confused by an inexperienced observer with a capercaillie hen, although the greyhen is much smaller. Blackgame occasionally hybridise with caper, red grouse and even pheasants, and such crossbreeds are not always easy to identify.

In former times blackgame occurred in many localities in England and Wales, as well as Scotland, but due to habitat changes, modern farming, land drainage, and to a lesser extent inconsiderate shooting, its range south of the Border is now greatly restricted. In Europe, where it takes a slightly different form, it is found in many of the wooded mountainous areas up to 6,000 ft, and also at sea level as in the Low Countries. Most populations are declining and in some countries the small colonies remaining must be doomed. Scientific investigations are taking place at international level. In Britain there are hopes that the population is at present more stable; but landowners are nevertheless concerned, not complacent.

Blackgame habitat includes the wooded fringe of moorland rather than the open moors. It is a bird of interface between grassland or moor and woodlands – a proportion of trees or shrubs appear to be an essential requirement provided they do not form too dense a stand. Blackgame may also be found on upland farms where they will frequent oat crops, rushy meadows and old pastures. But where agriculture becomes more productive, and modern dairy farms and silage crops take over, these grouse diminish.

Their food varies greatly according to the seasons, but is predominantly vegetable: it includes heather, pine shoots, berries, catkins – especially of birch – buds, grasses, seeds, cereals and many other plant items. Like caper, in certain circumstances they can cause damage to young forestry plantations. The young chicks feed on insects such as ants and also spiders.

Blackgame are promiscuous: there is no pair bond. The sexes only meet for copulation during the somewhat strange gatherings called leks, which often take place in traditional arenas about mid-March, continuing until mid-May. Here, beginning in the early hours of the morning and repeated in the late evening, the cocks – with swollen necks and distended wattles – go through ritual displays and dances which are sufficiently curious to have been frequently filmed and televised. In the Soviet Union two hundred birds have been observed at a lek; elsewhere, depending on the density of birds in the area, about ten males is more usual. Solitary cocks that do not visit leks also display. There is sometimes a smaller autumn lek.

Nests are made in heaths or scattered woods; 6–10 eggs of pale, buff, lightly spotted with reddish-brown, are laid usually from early May onwards. The cock takes no part in nest building, incubation or caring for the brood, and the hen unfortunately has a reputation of being a poor mother. Nest predation is often severe.

Blackcock have a number of calls, but the dove-like bubbling song of the male "roo-kooing", which can carry a long way and is heard chiefly in the spring, is one of the most typical.

In early August the old cocks will still be moulting and tend to stay in fairly dense cover such as old heather, bracken and rushes. The young will only be beginning to change from their reddish-brown coat to their full plumage of blue-black and white; the distinctive lyre-shaped tails will not be properly grown.

The open season begins some days later than for grouse, but even then they are by no means mature and the hens are often spared during a grouse drive. Blackgame fly faster than grouse, though with a slower wing beat. They are also heavier – an adult cock weighing from 3 lb 8 oz to over 4 lb, and a greyhen from 2 lb 4 oz to 3 lb.

As winter approaches flocks are often formed – consisting usually of one or other sex, or with one sex greatly predominating.

Black grouse are not easy to drive, and cannot be treated or managed like red grouse. The latter live largely in a world of heather which is uncomplicated in so far as the vegetation is concerned, though great skill is required to manage it correctly. Blackgame require a more complex habitat: and – once it is lost – to restore the correct balance of forest edge and open moor, perhaps with components of pasture, scrubland and marsh woven into the pattern, is not easy. Unfortunately in this material age it would be totally uneconomic.

Blackcock displaying

RED GROUSE

Lagopus lagopus scoticus

Plate X

THE red grouse – long famed by overseas sportsmen as being unique to our country – was at one time also classified as the only true British species of bird. Now the taxonomists have decided that it is a race of the Scandinavian willow grouse, despite the fact that it lives almost entirely on heather. In all other respects, however, it is distinctive: there is a charisma surrounding grouse and grouse shooting that is probably unrivalled in any other comparable form of hunting. It existed long before the Press dubbed the opening date "the Glorious Twelfth", a term not used by the guns: long before birds were flown from one end of the island to the other to be roasted for dinner that same night.

Grouse first caught the attention of the southern sportsmen in the latter half of the nineteenth century, when it was discovered more or less by accident that muirburn – or the burning of heather by the shepherds – was increasing the grouse stocks as well as benefiting the sheep. This happened only a decade or so after the breech-loading gun, invented by a Frenchman, had been further developed and popularised by English gunsmiths. Grouse driving on Lord Walsingham's moors in Yorkshire was in vogue by the 1860's, and by this time the new rail links to the North had made possible a faster and more comfortable journey than by stage coach. The demand for grouse shooting increased rapidly, and the money that the Sassenachs brought to the none-too-wealthy graziers soon caused moor management to be taken seriously. Today the red grouse are an even greater asset to the moors, and can be as valuable as the sheep. If they are properly husbanded, the two can be complementary.

Grouse nest among the heather, laying a clutch of about eight reddish-brown mottled eggs. The size of the clutch and the viability of the eggs are related to the nutrient content of the heather eaten by the hen during the laying period. If it is growing well it will be good; if it has been dried or killed by harsh winds and frost, it will be poor. In turn the stamina of the chicks will be largely determined by the quality of the eggs and the size of their yolk reserves, in spite of the fact that for the first few days the chicks will be feeding on insects. The young are cared for by both parents.

Heather condition – and therefore grouse nutrition – is improved by burning strips or patches of the moor on a rotation every ten years or so, depending on the type of ground. The minerals in the soil also have an effect on the nutritive quality of the vegetation – limestone being richer than granite, for example. On well-managed moors, with high-quality heather containing a good proportion of tender new shoots, grouse can normally provide a surplus of young birds, so that about 30 to 50 per cent can be harvested. By contrast, over-burning and heavy grazing by sheep can result in the replacement of the essential heather by rough grasses which are unpalatable to grouse, causing their numbers to decline.

Male grouse are highly territorial and, unlike partridges, will defend the boundaries of their territory. The older birds take up their territories first, and the courting of females cannot occur until this has been effected. The aggressiveness of the cock and the size of the ground he takes obviously influences the number of birds that a moor can hold. The density of these territories varies from season to season – the fluctuating numbers being partly governed by cycles. Parasitic worms, called strongyles, are sometimes found in huge numbers in the intestines of red grouse, and recent research suggests that at times the numbers of worms can become high enough to affect the grouse stocks and be responsible for this cyclic tendency. Grouse can, therefore, be in a state of decline even when their food supply is good. The worms do not multiply in the body of the grouse but are picked up individually from the heather plants.

In some areas grouse chicks can be killed off by a tick-borne virus disease known as louping-ill, which also affects sheep. This is now the subject of intensive research.

For newcomers to the sport grouse shooting can be hazardous – or rather hazardous to the guns in the neighbouring butts. These are often sited in line up the side of a hill, and built of weathered granite topped with sods of heather. Grouse tend to approach rather silently, not necessarily well up and silhouetted against the sky, but often swirling and dipping low over the contours of the hill. Against a background of purple heather, bracken browns, stone greys and lichen greens, the butts can merge into their surroundings sufficiently for an inexperienced gun to swing through the line.

Grouse have about fifteen to twenty different calls, the best known being "bekking", a clear and rapidly repeated "g'bek, g'bek"; sometimes interpreted as "Go back"!

Red Grouse becking

M.J.PLEDGER.

HAZEL HEN

Tetrastes bonasia

Plate XI

THIS attractive little grouse, which is about the same size as a partridge, conforms to the typical family shape, except that its tail is somewhat longer than average and its feet are only partially feathered. The cock has a conspicuous black throat, bordered with white: the crown of his head is slightly crested. The hen is smaller with a whitish throat. In flight both sexes show the fairly broad black band which edges the tail. The sound of their whirring wings is distinctive, and a bird which flushes in the woods unseen is often recognised by an experienced hunter. When disturbed it rarely flies any great distance, invariably taking refuge half way up a tree as soon as possible. Perching is quite usual and at night hazel hens tend to roost in trees amongst thick foliage as protection against martens and other predators.

The hazel hen, or hazel grouse as it is sometimes called, is essentially an arboreal, forest-loving species occurring mainly in mixed woodlands, interspersed with shrub bogland and grassy areas. It also frequents mature stands of mixed spruce, and pure birch and hazel, in the wilder hill and mountain country as well as in suitably wooded plains. It is practically never found out on open range. During the summer and autumn it prefers to live in fairly open deciduous woods, moving to pine forests at the approach of winter so as to take advantage of the better shelter and be less visible to birds of prey. Apart from these seasonal movements the hazel hen is mostly a sedentary grouse. It is also secretive, elusive and adept at self-concealment. Both adults and chicks are extremely predator conscious. The adults are cautious in almost everything they do: rarely flying over open ground or straying far from safe cover. The goshawk is the main predator in many areas. At the first sign of danger the chicks will squat or freeze motionless in a tree.

The distribution of the species is rather local: its range stretching eastwards from Scandinavia to Kamchatka in the Soviet Union, northern China and parts of Japan, with scattered colonies in Central Europe and the Balkans. There are still some small populations of hazel grouse in France and Belgium.

The hazel grouse is monogamous, having a seasonal pair-bond. Its way of life – keeping to fairly dense cover and for some reason seeming to be particularly at risk to predators – produces a close relationship with its partner. Breeding territories are loosely established in the autumn, and actively claimed or reclaimed in the spring.

The simple nest is made on the ground and 8–12 eggs are laid – pale buff, spotted with brown. The cock takes no part in incubating or rearing the young and leads an independent life while the hen is sitting. Curiously he will sometimes return to accompany the brood after they have hatched.

The food of hazel grouse is mainly vegetarian, comprising leaves, buds, shoots, berries and seeds from their forest surroundings: birch, alder and hazel being particularly favoured. Some insects are taken – ants being one of the more common items of their diet. Like some other woodland grouse their summer foraging is usually on the ground and their winter feeding up in the trees.

Because of its general sporting qualities and the fine flavour of its white flesh, this little grouse has always been a favourite of the hunter and for many decades was shot too heavily in some countries. Although difficult to track down even with pointers – partly because they often sat in the trees – the birds were called fairly easily with a decoy whistle, often made from the wing bone of a Blackcock or a hollowed out pithy stem cut on the spot. This method is now illegal in most countries.

Apart from excessive hunting pressure hazel grouse have always been extremely vulnerable to any deterioration of their habitat, and not surprisingly have decreased greatly. Today, their highest density occurs in Finland, where the forest environment is reasonably stable and disturbance by humans somewhat less than in other parts of the world criss-crossed by crowds of tourists. Because of their ability to hide, accurate bird counts are difficult and one can but hope that there are perhaps slightly more hazel grouse sheltering in the woods than are officially recorded.

Pair of Hazel Grouse on woodland floor

PTARMIGAN

Lagopus mutus

Plate XII

THE word *ptarmigan* has Gaelic origins. The German name for the species – literally translated – is "alpine snow bird"; an apt description for a creature of desolate tundra and bleak mountain tops, though in its most northern range it is also to be found at sea level. The bird atlas shows its habitat circling the northern latitudes right round the world, coming as close to the Pole as 400 miles. There are ptarmigan in Scandinavia, Iceland, Greenland, arctic North America and the Soviet Union: there are also colonies in the Alps and the Pyrenees.

In Scotland ptarmigan are usually to be found above 2,500 feet in the wilder and more remote parts of the highlands: likely to be seen by deer stalkers rather than grouse shooters. They are at home on the rather barren ground of the high hills, among the broken rocks and scant vegetation of grasses, *vaccinium* and stunted shrubs. Except under the stress of hard weather they only infrequently occupy the same ground as red grouse, mainly because their environmental requirements are different.

The ptarmigan runs about with agility; nimbly scaling rocky inclines and broken ground. In most of its range it rarely comes across human beings and when it does it usually shows immediate alarm and hurtles away into the empty sky. It is a magnificent flier and will seem to rise vertically up a steep rock face with the greatest ease, and it will dip in and out of hollows and corries without apparent effort.

At nesting time and throughout the summer their plumage, when seen from above, blends perfectly with the grey-green, lichen covered boulders, the mosses, heathers, scrubby brown plants and patches of bare earth. In flight some of the white underparts and wing feathers are conspicuous. As winter approaches their salt-and-pepper colour changes gradually to a white coat, though pure white only occurs in the very cold seasons – the cock always retaining his scarlet wattle and the black patch between eye and beak. There are, in fact, three changes of coat and many variations of plumage. Ptarmigan can sometimes be seen dusting or bathing in the snow, as well as digging into it for their protection.

Like the red grouse ptarmigan are territorial – the cock defending his territory with a clear, rattling song, as well as threat calls. His more usual voice consists of a hoarse croak.

The food of ptarmigan includes heather, also the shoots, flowers and berries of bilberry, crowberry, the shoots of dwarf sallow, the buds and catkins of birch, and many other items of vegetation found at these altitudes. The diet is mainly vegetable, but some insects, such as cranefly, are taken.

Pairing commences from the end of February onwards – depending on weather conditions – and copulation takes place towards the end of April. The ptarmigan is monogamous. Nesting usually begins in early May: the average clutch varying from five to eight. The eggs are rather similar to those of the red grouse, but smaller, with a paler background and dark brown blotches. Nests are not infrequently robbed by gulls and hooded crows. The main hatch occurs during the third week in June. The young are very precocious, and capable of flying within two weeks.

Predators, which are especially troublesome during nesting, include golden eagles and foxes, though the latter tend to be rather scarce at high altitudes.

The ptarmigan's range is thought to be slowly contracting: possibly for climatic reasons, though some of it is due to human intervention – probably indirect more than direct. In the Cairngorms, for example, the birds have adapted quite well to increased disturbance from ski-ing.

The ptarmigan weighs a little less than a red grouse.

Ptarmigan shooting is one of the truest forms of hunting – particularly late in the season after the birds have assumed their winter plumage. The sportsman who goes after ptarmigan at this time of the year has to be fit, and prepared for intense cold, mists and snowstorms. That gifted highland naturalist Seton Gordon described the conditions:

"During the short days of December, when darkness closes in about the hills three hours after noon, the soft calling of the ptarmigan is singularly in keeping with their surroundings of grandeur. On such a day I have crossed through a wild hill-pass, and at the watershed have disturbed a large pack of these white grouse. The murmur of many snowy wings as the birds wheeled their way above my head from one hill face to another is a sound which will for long be retained as a highly prized gift of the high hills – given only to those who know and appreciate them in winter gloom as well as under a summer's sun."

Ptarmigan in winter plumage

WILLOW GROUSE

Lagopus lagopus

Plate XIII

As the red grouse has now been classified as a race of the willow grouse, the two are often merged under the same heading in modern textbooks. To add to the confusion of the layman, in North America the willow grouse is called the willow ptarmigan. From a distance it can, in fact, be almost indistinguishable from our European ptarmigan *Lagopus mutus*, though there are minor differences in the shape of the bill and the head markings. The altitude at which the birds are seen, the type of habitat and their calls are additional guides to identifying them correctly.

Between red and willow grouse there are also a number of differences: the red grouse does not turn white or nearly white in winter, and it is a bird of the open heather moors, whereas the willow grouse frequents mainly scrubland of willow, birch, alder and juniper, which provide its principal foods. However, in addition to living in mixed scrub country and various types of Arctic tundra, on some of the Norwegian inshore islands and in Newfoundland it also frequents heathlands. Unlike the red grouse it will sit in trees and shrubs to peck at buds and shoots in the winter time. So far as we know it does not suffer from either strongylosis disease or the louping ill virus which affect red grouse.

After the ptarmigan the willow grouse is the hardiest and most northerly of the *Tetraonidae*. Its range is circumpolar; through Scandinavia, the Soviet Union, Alaska, Canada, the Arctic Archipelago, Newfoundland and Greenland. There are a number of sub-species. Off the Norwegian coast there are limited movements between the various islands and the mainland, but on the whole the species is sedentary, except when the icing on the vegetation becomes severe and forces the birds to fly elsewhere to find food.

In addition to feeding on the tundra plants and scrub vegetation, it also eats bilberries and other *Vacciniums*, as well as the seeds and flowers of knotgrass. This is called "ripagrass" in Norway – ripa being the local name for willow grouse. The chicks will take insects during the first two weeks of life, also flowers, leaves and moss capsules.

The species is monogamous. When the spring thaw begins and the winter flocks break up, the cocks start to exhibit their territorial tendencies and pairing follows. Nests are usually made under a bush, beside a tree stump, among *vacciniums*, or heather in certain places. The eggs are not unlike those of red grouse – the clutch varying from 8–10. The male is at all times a solicitous parent and helps to care for the young. Although he takes no part in the incubation, according to an American naturalist he will sometimes make a separate nest of his own – near to the female's – so that he can come to her aid if she calls. Gulls and crows are frequent nest robbers, and his intervention is often needed.

For centuries willow grouse were quite an important food source for Lapps, Eskimos and Red Indians. Today they are usually hunted over dogs; in the late Autumn they can be difficult to pick out among the rocks and stones that their plumage resembles. They seem to understand the art of camouflage, and when moulting into their white winter plumage they are often to be found on stretches of open tundra where the cotton grass is bearing its white plumes. There may be other reasons for visiting these localities, but the change of coat is their main defence against their enemies. In summer when they are a brownish colour and merge with similar ground tones, they become comparatively tame. But in the spring, before they have completely moulted out their partly white winter dress, they are extremely suspicious and wary. During the moults they will hide away in birch and juniper scrub, which provides them with protective cover.

In the depths of winter they are particularly hard to see when perching in snow-laden branches. On a bright sunny day a hunter will sometimes recognise the dark shadow of a bird silhouetted on the snowy ground, before he makes out the bird itself – unless there is a movement of the eye or the black bill. Like other northern grouse, they will roost in holes and hollows in the snow, usually finding or excavating a new hole each night. Willow grouse have feathered legs and feet which help them walk across soft snow.

As to their table qualities, they are the least in demand of the grouse family. In winter the flesh of the old birds tends to be dark, dry and rather bitter, as a result of a diet which may be mainly of birch and willow twigs. In the autumn, however, when the young birds are feeding on fresh foliage, berries and insects, the flavour can be quite good. And camping in a Lapp hut hundreds of miles from civilisation – with most of ones rations in tins – a friend of mine assures me that the bird is an epicurean delight.

Willow Grouse in Autumn plumage

RUFFED GROUSE

Bonasa umbellus

Plate XIV

THE ruffed grouse ranks fourth in popularity with American hunters in the upland game category, after bobwhite quail, pheasant and mourning dove. Its white meat has a delicious flavour: it was always a favourite food of the Northern Indian tribes, and subsequently greatly appreciated by the early pioneers.

There are several sub-species and two colour phases: grey and reddish-brown. The grey phase being generally associated with northern areas of higher altitudes, and the brown phase with southern habitats and lower altitudes. It is suggested that the different colouring may be a protective adaptation to the type of woodland background: one being more easily hunted by raptors and another by mammalian predators, according to the denseness of the cover.

The ruffed grouse is one of the most widely distributed birds of North America – its range extends east and west from the Atlantic to the Pacific, and north and south from Alaska to Georgia. It can adapt to a variety of forest types, from temperate coniferous rain forest to relatively arid deciduous woodland. It survives better in hardwoods than conifers, preferably in stands of mixed ages – which can provide both winter and summer food, as well as useful breeding habitat. The highest densities are found where aspens and poplars grow well. Paper birch *Betula papyrifera* is another key component of a good habitat. Mixtures of hardwoods and conifers are even better than pure stands, and a good shrub understorey is vital for the drumming sites that are essential to the grouse. Small clearings, which will provide shrubs such as blackberries, wild raspberries, dogwoods, virburnums, thorns and so on are much favoured.

The ruffed grouse, although quite at home in the temperate south-eastern states, is well adapted to severe winter weather. Sometimes, the birds will roost beneath loose snow and remain there for several days. Rarely do they become frozen into a snowy tomb, but under such circumstances predation from mammals such as foxes can be high.

The species is polygamous: the male takes no part in caring for the brood. The femals are attracted to a cock by the sound of his "drumming" on a display site. Drumming can be heard all the year round, but the peak occurs in the spring – usually beginning before dawn. The noise advertises the male's presence in fairly dense cover where he would not easily be seen – both to prospective mates and to other males who might be intent on establishing territories.

The cock usually stands on a suitable log, which he grips firmly with his claws – his tail braced against its surface – while he indulges in his drumming. The noise – a dull throbbing sound that one observer described as like the starting up of a one cylinder gas engine – results from air compression produced by the strong forward wing beats. These start quite slowly and rapidly speed up. If another male intrudes, the "drummer" will strut towards him with tail fanned out and ruff spread, hissing and generally looking threatening. A strutting display also takes place prior to copulation with females. Not surprisingly when cock grouse use a favoured log regularly and its use is continued – perhaps by their progeny – for successive seasons, the site becomes known to predators and casualties result.

The nests are made near the edges of plantations or clearings, usually at the foot of trees or beside logs. About 10 or 11 brownish eggs are laid; the colour varying from light tea to chestnut. The chicks fly 10–12 days after hatching. When they are about 12 or more weeks old, the families begin to break up and the juvenile birds disperse. The basic food of ruffed grouse chicks for the first 10 days or so consists of insects such as ants, sawflies, beetles, spiders, grasshoppers, various caterpillars and so on. Being mainly a woodland species the adult diet is composed largely of leaves – particularly aspen and poplar – twigs, catkins, berries, fruits and buds, but some insects are taken.

The ruffed grouse is a challenging game bird to shoot: most of the time the sportsman is in fairly thick cover and the bird's ability to twist about in flight and place a tree between itself and the hunter makes it a very difficult target. After the first frosts, when there has been some leaf fall and visibility in the woods is improved, conditions can be a little easier.

The birds weigh between 1 lb and 1 lb 10 oz – the sexes being rather similar, except that the hens are a little smaller, with shorter tails, and slightly different tail-feather markings.

One curious habit of the ruffed grouse – a species which does not undertake any normal migratory movements – is its "crazy flight." When indulging in this phenomenon the young grouse will occasionally fly quite long distances into built-up areas of towns: sometimes crashing into buildings. The reasons for this erratic behaviour are not yet properly understood.

Ruffed Grouse in Autumn woods

M.J. PLEDGER

SAGE GROUSE

Centrocercus urophasianus

Plate XV

THE sage grouse or sage hen not unexpectedly lives in a world of sagebrush. Wild sage, *Artemesia*, is to this game bird very much what heather is to the red grouse. It provides almost all its requirements – nutritious food, nesting and escape cover. As it is evergreen, fairly tough and tall enough to stand above the snow in localities with hard winters, it offers useful shelter as well as food.

For the spring strutting grounds the birds prefer relatively open sage cover; for nesting they choose plants up to two feet high, and for brood raising they favour big sagebrush where the growth is patchy, with about one-third shrub cover. Throughout the year three-quarters of their diet will consist of sage – the remainder being herbaceous legumes and weeds, and insects such as grasshoppers when they are available.

Sage grouse were at one time common throughout most of the western and inter-mountain States wherever sagebrush was found. In some they were the main upland game species. However, from the early 1900s overgrazing and drought degraded the habitat and the grouse declined. Recently there has been some recovery and they are once again quite an important quarry in Wyoming, Montana, Colorado, Idaho, Nevada and further west. But as extensive areas are still being cleared for irrigated croplands, and the use of herbicides is steadily increasing, the sagebrush and its grouse must continue to dwindle.

In the late winter, often when the snow is still lying, the sage grouse will begin to leave their wintering ranges – sometimes a hundred miles away – and return along established routes to their strutting grounds. Here the curious courtship displays are performed to attract the females. From February onwards – depending on the area – the build-up of birds assembling at the leks intensifies. In due course, with the males taking the centre of the stage and the females waiting in the wings, the complicated systems of social hierarchy are sorted out and matings eventually take place. The species is polygamous. It is said that the sage grouse has the most complex lek social structure of all. As many as 400 males have been observed at one gathering; and in one recorded case three-quarters of all the copulations were performed by only five of the strongest males – the master cocks or alpha birds.

Like the prairie chicken the male sage grouse has air sacs beside its neck, which it inflates and deflates during its display – the bellows effect producing its own strange mating call. After mating the hens leave the strutting grounds for suitable nesting areas. The average clutch is 7–8: the eggs are grey-green, thickly spotted with reddish-brown.

The chicks feed on a variety of insects for the first few days, then change to weedy forbs and cultivated crops such as clovers and alfalfa – or lucerne – until finally at about three months their staple diet is sagebrush. An important component of the habitat when the young are growing up is moisture in some form, either natural water, irrigated land, or areas where the foods can supply juices or fluids. As the summer progresses the need for moisture or fresh green plant material increases, and the broods will move to find it.

Although this game bird is sought after by hunters, the majority do not rate it very highly as a quarry species. It presents an easy target and rises from the ground with a lumbering take-off, though it may then gather speed quite rapidly and fly a long distance. In flight the white feathering under the wings contrasts sharply with the blackish abdomen. When on the wing it will "chuckle", though not quite as clearly as the sharp tail.

An unexpected bonus of the sage environment – in so far as the grouse is concerned – is that it gives the bird's flesh a strong tangy flavour, which some hunters describe as only just tolerable. Young birds bagged in the late summer when they are eating foods other than, or in addition to, the fundamental sage, are more palatable – particularly if they are drawn as soon as shot. The sage grouse is the largest and heaviest member of the North American grouse family, the cock weighing up to 8 lb: the hen is only half the weight.

Pair of Sage Grouse – Male displaying

GREATER PRAIRIE CHICKEN

Tympanuchus cupido

Plate XVI

As a form of sexual display, challenge and invitation to prelude the breeding season, sharp-tailed grouse have their dancing grounds, ruffed grouse their drumming logs, sage grouse their strutting grounds and prairie chickens their booming grounds.

Some years ago we reared a few prairie chickens at the Game Conservancy as the result of a wager with an American professor, who suggested that they would be too difficult. When the breeding season came round we were delighted to see and hear the cock bird going through his ritual performance, with tail erected, neck or pinnae feathers raised and spread, and his bright orange air sacs ballooning out. As these sacs inflated and deflated a loud hollow booming noise was emitted, greatly puzzling the townspeople until we explained what it was. In due course the B.B.C. came to record our exotic prairie bird.

On the wild grasslands of North America the performance is probably even more dramatic: the booming starts before dawn and is accompanied by a rapid stamping of the bird's feet which creates an additional drumming noise. The booming across the open ground is said to be audible at a distance of two miles or more – the sound having been variously described as the noise produced by blowing across the top of a Coca Cola bottle or the resonant tone of an orchestral kettle drum.

Should an enemy appear in the sky the whole pantomime can cease abruptly. A witness has described how he was watching the male's antics when a snowy owl flew over. In a split second the air sacs emptied, the tall neck plumes disappeared and the bird became "a squatting brownish lump – almost invisible."

At one time these grouse were numerous in all the prairie States from the Canadian border down to Texas. They were one of the species which at first benefited as the virgin prairies were settled and broken up into grain fields – the cereals providing valuable extra winter food. Such was the increase that for a time they were accused of destroying crops, and shot as pests. They were shipped to meat markets all over the country. In 1871 the traders in Chicago alone sold 513,000 "prairie grouse". Even if this figure included sharp-tails, the figure was substantial. But in time, as the cereal production increased and the proportion of native grassland decreased, the habitat degenerated until it was no longer suitable for prairie chickens. The process had turned full circle. Farming today has continued to squeeze them out, and reduce the population to a tiny proportion of what it was even before the great upsurge. The two sub-species, the lesser and Attwater's prairie chicken have declined even more sharply. The Eastern race, the heath hen, is extinct.

The greater prairie chicken is now mainly confined to Kansas, Oklahoma, Nebraska and South Dakota, apart from a few patchy outlying colonies. The bluestem prairies of Eastern Kansas constitute the heart of its present range; the best areas containing natural grasslands and cultivated feed crops in the ratio of two to one. In some areas the decline has for the time being been halted. Game reserves have been established, hunting restricted and in the States where winters are hard, feeding stations have been set up and game crops planted such as buckwheat, sorghum and sun-flowers. In snowy areas the prairie chickens are migratory – moving south when winter sets in and returning in the early spring. Elsewhere the birds are sedentary.

In the early summer prairie fires have always been a problem, destroying both nests and breeding stock. In the fall these fires scorch away food and cover – exposing the survivors to predators. Controlled burning in the early spring, of course, improves tall, dense grassland, and helps to re-establish and invigorate valuable plants.

The nests, which are generally to be found within half a mile to a mile of the booming grounds are usually well hidden in thick vegetation. About 12 eggs are laid, olive coloured and speckled with brown. Hatching takes place early in June, and when available the hens take their chicks to pastures containing fresh greenstuff such as forbs. In the heat of the day they will seek out shrubs or trees for shade. The male plays no part in raising the brood, and soon after the courtship is over he goes into retirement prior to moulting.

Although grasshoppers are eaten in quantity when available, the prairie chicken is mainly a vegetarian. Grain is an important item, acorns are also taken, and in the late spring soybeans are a favourite food.

As a sporting bird its performance is the subject of controversy: most hunters assert that it is not a particularly difficult bird to shoot. But it is much appreciated on the table, particularly in the late summer when the young birds are plump and well flavoured. A cock would weigh 2–2½ lb.

On the whole the prairie chicken – known to hunters as "old yellowlegs" – is a remarkable game bird. For the sportsmen of the shrinking prairies it occupies the same place as the ruffed grouse does for people living in wooded country, in their affection if not in numbers.

Prairie chicken on booming ground – Male

M.J.PLEDGER.

WILD TURKEY

Meleagris galloparvo sp.

Plate XVII

THE wild turkey is indigenous to North America.

When the Pilgrim Fathers arrived on the New England coast in 1620 the turkeys in their "feathered armour of glistening bronze" – thus described by A. C. Bent – would have been among the first gamebirds to have been seen and hunted. Wild turkey was served at the first Thanksgiving, and subsequently became the traditional dish. Benjamin Franklin said that he would have much preferred this magnificent bird to have been chosen as the national emblem of the United States, rather than the baldheaded eagle, which he described as "of bad moral character.". The existence of wild turkeys was first reported by the early Spanish explorers. By 1517 birds had been domesticated by the natives of Yucatan: in 1524 some stock reached England. There is some confusion as to why they were called "turkeys". One theory is that they were thought to be a type of guineafowl, some of which had earlier been imported from Turkey: another that the word resembled one of their calls.

Not all the native Indians killed wild turkeys for meat – to some tribes it was taboo. Others used the feathers in their head dresses and some of the bones as needles for stitching leather. A number of the tribes performed dances based on the movements of the displaying turkeys. In Europe in the days of ragtime the rather ridiculous turkey trot was in vogue.

At one time different races of the wild turkey occurred from Southern Mexico to New England and even Canada, but the steady erosion of its forest habitat, combined with uncontrolled hunting in the early days greatly reduced its range. Originally it was an easy bird to kill, but after centuries of being hunted it became sharp-eyed, wild, elusive and secretive. Great expertise and patience is now required to outwit them. Experienced sportsmen stalking them or shooting from hides use camouflaged apparel and blacken their faces. Where spring shooting is permitted decoy calls are often used to attract the birds to within range; nationwide competitions being held, with prestigious trophies awarded for the most lifelike callers. Depending on the State either rifles or shotguns may be used – the former usually in open forest, the latter where the cover is close.

A male tom or gobbler can weigh up to 30 lb; a hen averaging 6–10 lb.

To the dedicated American hunter the wild turkey is more than just something for the cook pot; it is a rare prize. For many sportsmen, it is enough to kill one in a season: even one in a lifetime. Although, like the pheasant, the turkey prefers to run rather than fly, when it does take wing it can reach a speed of over 50 m.p.h.

Good turkey habitat consists of open, mature woodlands – ideally mixtures of oak and pine, with suitable trees for roosting, and providing fruit and mast such as acorns, beech nuts, pecans and pine kernels. The birds also graze on grasses and legumes, which in turn harbour grasshoppers and other insects that are much sought after by the young birds. In other habitats they will eat prickly pear fruits, grapes, juniper berries – whatever is available.

No turkeys will thrive without nearby water in some form; woodlands that border streams or contain springs or seeps being much favoured. As a defence against predators the birds like to roost on branches over water. The species is polygamous and in the breeding season a harem may consist of a gobbler and five or six hens. The selection of mates takes place in February or March after a great deal of displaying – with tails fanned out and wing quills drooping and rattling – usually in a woodland arena. The gobblers will sometimes indulge in a bloody combat for up to two hours, the loser occasionally getting killed. Only the strongest will succeed in winning a mate, and some unsuccessful males never manage to copulate in the whole of their lives.

The incubation period lasts 26–28 days. The clutch averages 10–15: the eggs varying from cream to buff, sprinkled with reddish dots. Wild turkeys are among the species that indulge in hen to chick conversation *before* the eggs hatch. It is thought that the chicks within the shell thus acquire the mother's "language" and more easily learn to stay together after hatching. After six days the young can fly and after two weeks they can go up to roost, at first sheltering under the mother's wings.

Their enemies are numerous: many clutches are lost and many chicks killed in the first few days of life. Predators include crows, certain owls and other birds-of-prey, the red fox, bobcats, skunks, raccoons, domestic dogs and cats, and not surprisingly with such a large quarry – poachers.

Many birds live to the age of six years; some to ten. The age of gobblers can be judged by the length of the beard or tuft which adorns the chest and can be up to ten inches in length. Old hens also have these tufts, but they are considerably shorter.

Wild Turkey displaying in woodland

M.J.PLEDGER.

GREAT BUSTARD

Otis tarda

Plate XVIII

THERE are several species of bustards: the two best known being the magnificent great bustard, once resident in England, and the houbara bustard of the desert, not so long ago the quarry of princely Arab falconers mounted on horseback, though now more often pursued in Land Rovers and declining as a result.

In England information about the bustard is somewhat anecdotal and fragmentary, but we know that the last specimen to breed was recorded in Suffolk around the early 1830's. Until they died out they had inhabited the brecklands of East Anglia, extensive chalk downs and wild grassy country: all habitats that have now dwindled, altered greatly or are subject to the type of human disturbance with which the bustard cannot live. The great bustard needs space around it.

It is the largest European land bird capable of flight: a record male shot in Spain in 1890 weighed 40 lb, though 20–25 lb is more usual, with the hen weighing 8 to 9 lb. A few years ago when I was tracking bustards on a wet spring day in Hungary, I found some footprints which had crossed a wet, boggy path. Such was the weight of the bird, that his great feet had sunk several inches into the earth. Bustards are extremely wary and difficult to approach; however, one day – with a fierce gale searing across the open steppes – we accidentally disturbed a feeding flock. They took to the air at once: but even with their huge, powerful wings they could not fight the strength of the wind and were blown right over our heads at a low altitude. It was a stirring sight.

The male bird is renowned for a strange and picturesque breeding ritual in which, by suddenly displaying the undersides of his wings and tail, the buff coloured suitor seems to envelop himself in a frothy white cloak of softest plumes. At the same time his neck sac becomes greatly distended. Another feature of this eccentric bird is his bristling moustache of fine white feathers.

Bustards are monogamous in the wild: the hen alone incubates the clutch of 2 or 3 eggs and broods the chicks. The young feed largely on insects – grasshoppers being a favourite. The adult diet consists mainly of vegetable matter, including cereals, clovers, peas, brassicas and grasses, but some animal matter is taken such as earthworms, frogs and even field voles.

Two or three countries have now established experimental breeding farms for bustards, used for study and for modest attempts at restocking depleted areas. But the species is not particularly easy to propagate: the cocks are usually not fertile until they are four or five years of age and the small egg output hampers efforts to produce stock in reasonable numbers.

In Central Europe their nesting casualties in the wild are invariably heavy. Lucerne is a favourite cover crop – the height of the plants allows them initially to look through the top of the greenery, and as it grows they become securely hidden. But unfortunately cutting takes place at almost the same time as hatching, and severe losses occur. If they nest in cereals the disturbance caused by spraying forces them to desert, and late combining kills the young bustards that are not yet able to fly. Even the electricity pylons constitute a hazard, for they seem to be strung across the sky at almost exactly the height at which the birds choose to fly. As a result many bustards are killed.

In both Hungary and Spain – due to the interest of the owners of hunting preserves and State funds – the decline of the bustard populations has at present been slowed down, though one wonders for how long? Fortunately, in Spain the best bustard areas in the province of Caceres consist mostly of very poor land, which owing to its rocky terrain does not permit the use of mechanised farming methods, nor warrant the application of pesticides and other chemicals. For a time the birds have a sanctuary. But apart from a few pockets of land where agriculture has stood still, the future for the bustard is not good.

At one time trophy hunting, when only the cocks were shot, caused a sexual imbalance resulting in infertile eggs being laid. But this lesson has now been learned.

In spite of dedicated conservation measures the great bustard – a species that has been with us for at least a million years – has not learned to adapt to the present century. As the wild open spaces continue to be tamed, most populations of the quaint *Otis tarda* continue to dwindle.

Great Bustard – female on nest

M.J.PLEDGER.

MALLARD

Anas platyrhynchos

Plate XIX

I T is possible that the mallard was the first bird ever to have been domesticated by man – long before the chicken. It was kept in captivity by both Egyptians and Chinese several centuries before Christ. To many sportsmen wild duck simply means mallard. It is undoubtedly the most widespread and best known duck in the Northern Hemisphere. Its breeding range in Europe is extensive, from southern Greece to Lapland. It is a partial migrant; most temperate areas have a resident population, which is augmented in winter by an influx of northerly breeding birds, from Iceland, Scandinavia and the Western Soviet Union.

The mallard is a successful species, probably because it is adaptable, generally tolerant of man's activities, and an opportunistic and almost omnivorous feeder. Its tastes range from the bread crusts scattered about in urban parks to shed barley grains after harvest; acorns, slugs, frosted potatoes, even small frogs. In watery surroundings it will feed on green pondweeds and seeds, and inverte-brates such as snails, leeches, shrimps, caddis and worms. The young need plenty of animal protein early in life. Mallard will dabble for aquatic food in the shallows; where it is deeper they will up-end and occasionally dive just below the surface. They usually feed at night, flighting in to the selected area at dusk, and leaving at dawn for protected waters – often large lakes – where they can roost undisturbed in the centre, or on islands or mudspits, safe from foxes and other predators.

They are equally at home on small ponds as in water-filled ditches or streams, rivers, watercress beds, moorland tarns, wet gravel pits, reservoirs and natural lakes. The larger stretches of water are used mainly as winter roosts; for breeding they prefer smaller, more secluded sites, with suitable nesting cover not too far from the water's edge.

Pair formation starts in the autumn, and during courtship two or more drakes will squabble aggressively over a single duck: the chase often taking place in the air. Females are also frequently pursued when they come off their nests to feed and swim. Copulation, which takes place on the water, can be violent and the duck can be virtually raped and set on by a succession of males. Sometimes after several duckings she will actually be drowned. Under more normal circumstances, however, a few watery quacks will bubble up from below the surface, and the duck suffer no permanent ill-effects.

The nest, lined with soft down and feathers, is usually made on the ground in marginal vegetation, grasses, scrub or woodland, though sometimes it will be found in a tree such as a pollarded willow. The clutch generally consists of 10–12 eggs: pale grey-green in colour. The ducklings are taken to the water on hatching, and reared in shallow areas rich in vegetation and aquatic animal life. Brood production is patchy: some mothers seem to rear all their young: others only one or two. The average is rather low, and perhaps to compensate the mallard has the longest breeding season of any European duck, nesting in ten months of the year where conditions are suitable.

Centuries ago the Dutch, who made a successful business of catching mallard in their commercial decoys, learned to increase the breeding density by providing nesting baskets, woven of reed or osier, and set up on stakes just above the surface of the water. Here the occupants were safe from foxes, and sharp-eyed crows. When making a television film on the subject we spent hours watching the fluffy newly-hatched ducklings splashing down one at a time from the baskets to the water below. Pike, incidentally, will voraciously snap up baby ducklings from the surface.

The male takes no part in incubation or brood rearing, but usually remains in the vicinity until the hatch is complete. Soon afterwards he undergoes his eclipse moult, hiding away in protective cover while he is vulnerable to his enemies.

For ten years or so, when I lived in a cottage beside some flooded, reed-fringed brick pits, my everyday life was virtually shared with about thirty pairs of mallard and their broods. My conservation measures mistakenly included some feeding, in return for which the ducks invaded and ruined the garden. During the course of this enforced relationship, one duckling – abandoned in the nest and revived in the airing cupboard – became imprinted on me. It accompanied us on holiday to a Norfolk estuary and swam delightedly "at heel" behind my dinghy. When I dug up ragworms as fishing bait it regularly contrived to knock the pot over and eat as many as it could before I intervened. In time it evolved a special feeding call – previously unknown to science, one might think – which was produced whenever I appeared with the bait pot.

Incidentally, the familiar deep reedy quack is only uttered by the adult female: the male can but muster a rather subdued and insignificant little grating noise, more suitable to some shy creature lurking in the sedges and King-cups than to this chauvinistic bird.

Mallard Drake by the water's edge

M.J.PLEDGER.

TEAL

Anas crecca

Plate XX

THE teal is one of the dabbling ducks; what the Americans sometimes call a puddleduck. There are a number of teal species in different parts of the world. *Anas crecca* is the smallest of the European ducks, being only a quarter the weight of a mallard: it is also one of our most abundant species. The bright chestnut head of the male and the broad green eye stripe make it very distinctive: in its eclipse moult, of course, it closely resembles the female.

Their flight is rapid and a flock of teal will sometimes wheel and turn in unison like waders. The collective term for them is a "spring" of teal, probably because when they are disturbed they take off by springing up into the air almost vertically. They are very mobile ducks undertaking long seasonal migrations. Birds ringed in Britain are often recovered as far afield as the Leningrad region of the Soviet Union. They breed in most countries in mid-Western Europe, including Britain: the highest concentrations are in Scandinavia and the Western and Central parts of the Soviet Union. Large numbers arrive in the British Isles from the East to winter in our islands. They seem to be susceptible to cold weather and are often forced to retreat southwards during hard winters.

The teal could be called a talkative duck, often chuckling conversationally and when grouped in flocks communicating with short sweet whistles. When the drake is courting he will call to his mate with a low double whistle.

When not advertising their presence by talking, they tend to be secretive; preferring areas where there is plenty of suitable cover where they can feed, shelter and hide. Although for most of the year they are mainly birds of sheltered freshwater habitats such as reedy pools and quiet streams, in winter they are also found on coastal marshes and saltwater estuaries.

Most, but not all, of their feeding is done at night, while wading in shallow water among the marginal plants – pond weeds and sedges. Here they filter out small items of vegetable matter. They are mainly seed-eaters. They are also fond of grain, and teal in warmer countries will visit rice fields. Animal food includes insects, worms, molluscs and small crustaceans.

By day, rather like mallard, they will roost on large stretches of sheltered water or on mudbanks.

Their nests are usually well concealed in sedges or scrub – sometimes among heather or out on marshlands; they do not always nest close to water. Eight to ten eggs are laid – pale stone to light greenish-buff in colour. Some of the males remain with the females during hatching, and some assist in attending the young. But most cock teal will leave their mates when they start incubating and gather in large flocks ready for the moult. These flocks are sometimes joined by unsuccessful breeding females.

This attractive little duck has always been a favourite with wildfowlers. It affords difficult shooting, particularly when indulging in its sudden spring from the water – rocketing up with dripping wings. It is an agile quarry which can surprise a gun almost anywhere: on reed-fringed pools, moorland flashes, bogs, fenland dykes and around the edges of large lakes. It has a succulent flesh which most people think is even better than the mallard. Alexander Innes Shand writing on game cooking at the turn of the century described the teal as "the gem of the duck tribe and the jewel of the spit." To a "fowler the distinctive noise of teals" wings crossing the night sky overhead – perhaps comparable to the clear musical whistle of the wigeon coming out of the dark – is one of the most evocative of nocturnal sounds.

Cock Teal by reeds and wild mint

M.J.PLEDGER

WIGEON

Anas penelope

Plate XXI

LIKE mallard and teal, wigeon are dabbling or surface-feeding ducks. They are one of the more common species, and their musical *whee-oo* call – rather similar to the noise produced from the tin-whistles in Christmas crackers – is a familiar sound on coastal marshes at night, as well as on other occasions such as courting. The French call the wigeon the *canard siffleur*.

The main weight of wigeon in the British Isles are winter visitors, but it also breeds in Scotland and northwards to Iceland, Scandinavia and the northern parts of the Soviet Union. Few birds breed south of 55°. Although there are some earlier arrivals, the peak build-up of the winter visitors coming from these areas occurs in October. Other populations fly south to Japan, southern China, Burma, India and Mediterranean areas.

Although wigeon are found on lakes some distance from the coast, they are really saltwater ducks. They are mainly vegetarians, and at one time their staple food was *zostera marina* or eelgrass, which grew in quantity on tidal mudflats. The older generation of wildfowlers and naturalists will probably remember when, in the 1930s, this sea grass was attacked by a disease which destroyed vast tracts of it. This had a particularly dramatic effect on the wintering Brent geese for which it was an essential food. Fortunately the wigeon proved to be more adaptable, managing to find other things to eat on the saltings as well as turning to new inland feeding areas. As more reservoirs were built they began to use them as roosts from which to go foraging on nearby pastures. Wigeon bills – like those of some geese – have serrated edges which enable them to shear blades of grass effectively and closely. In addition to grazing they take plant material such as flote grass off the surface of the water, and go beachcombing for marine worms, molluscs and small crustaceans. Seaweed, particularly *enteromorpha*, is an important wigeon food. They eat grain, including rice, and also some plant stems and roots. They will associate with other birds such as swans, Brent geese and even coot, to eat the left-over foods excavated and brought to the surface by them.

By the end of March many wigeon have paired. During the courtship proceedings ceaseless *wheeoo's* are uttered by the amorous males in attendance while the selection is being considered. The ornithologist Heinroth tells us that once mated the pairs are very united – the drakes not having the promiscuous tendencies of many other duck species.

The nest is made on the ground in fairly thick cover such as bracken, rough herbage or heather, not always adjacent to water. Nests have occasionally been found in the middle of grouse moors. Six to eight light buff or cream coloured eggs are laid. During incubation the drake or "cock", as male wigeon and teal are more usually called, remains in the vicinity of the nest, usually rejoining his family when they have been taken to the nearest water after hatching.

Depending on where and on what they have been feeding wigeon can make very good eating, and are often the mainstay of the shore gunner. The cock wigeon weighs about 1 lb 10 oz – about 1 lb less than a drake mallard. Wigeon are faster fliers than mallard and often come by in tight bunches, twisting and turning in flight. By day they will often roost off-shore in great rafts, sleeping quite peacefully even in a choppy sea. As T. A. Coward wrote: "looking like undulating collections of floating wrack as the birds rise and fall on the waves."

This habit of roosting out at sea, which they adopt particularly when their feeding grounds have been disturbed, can provide the dwindling band of punt-gunners with a difficult quarry to stalk, except early in the season when they have just arrived: difficult, unless the tide, the wind, the state of the sea and perhaps of the moon and the clouds are just right.

Cock Wigeon in reeds at water's edge

M.J.PLEDGER

CANADA GOOSE

Branta canadensis

Plate XXII

THE Canada goose is a native of North America, with not less than twelve sub-species to provide variety. They are probably the best known and most widely distributed species of wildfowl in these regions. From the Atlantic across to the Pacific, and from the Gulf of Mexico to the Arctic, at some season or other Canada geese can usually be seen or heard. When flying long distances they invariably keep to their well known "V" formations or an oblique line abreast, but for shorter flights they more often form loose, irregular patterns in the sky. The stirring, resonant honking of the flying skeins will be familiar to most people: when feeding they tend to indulge in more muted, conversational honking and gabbling.

Notwithstanding its rather stark livery, the Canada is certainly a strikingly ornamental bird. It was said to have been introduced into England to grace the lakes and parklands of estate owners – and even to enhance our towns – as early as the reign of King Charles II. In due course the geese bred wild and increased their range, though the colonisation of new areas was as much due to landowners putting down stock as to the birds spreading out on their own. The introduced population is largely sedentary, though some birds undertake moult migrations of up to 250 miles in preparation for their vulnerable flightless period.

During the last three decades the numbers of Canada geese rapidly increased in places to pest proportions. From a British census figure of 3,500 in 1953 the population had increased to 20,000 by 1976 and has been rising at about 6 per cent each year. Whilst they normally do no great harm grazing on the shoots of cereals, when they pull up the kernels and extensively puddle damp ground the damage they cause can be considerable. A heavy deposit of droppings can also badly foul the land.

Canada geese are an adaptable species; they are long lived and have few predators. They have also learned to tolerate people within reason, although there is a great difference between birds resident on an English farm – accustomed to tractors and farm workers – and the wild isolated flocks in the wastes of Northern Canada. Here they are exceptionally wary and alert, always posting sentinels when feeding to give the rest of the flock warning of approaching danger. They will differentiate at once between man-made noise such as a paddle touching the side of a canoe, and a natural sound like a deer stepping on a dry branch or a turtle splashing into the water.

In their native continent the utilisation of different habitats is very wide, from prairies and semi-desert regions to the tundras of the far north. In England they prefer freshwater lakes and marshes, and the surrounding pasture and park land.

They feed largely on pastures, though in spring and summer they will turn to cereal crops. According to the locality they have adopted they will also take a variety of other vegetable foods, such as marsh grasses and aquatic plants, and a proportion of animal foods including insects, molluscs and small crustacea. They normally feed during the day, but if persecuted they will resort to night feeding.

Canada geese pair for life, and for most of the year are gregarious – sometimes associating with grey geese. They will interbreed with other geese, particularly Barnacles, but only hybrids with other *branta* species are fertile. Occasionally they interbreed with swans.

They prefer to nest on scrub covered islands, or in suitable cover close to water. In North America they occasionally nest in trees, using old osprey or heron nests high above the ground. Five or six whitish eggs are laid in April to be incubated for 28 or 29 days by the female alone. Both parents, however, will tend the young.

The meat of the Canada goose is delicious to eat – possibly the tastiest of all wild geese. But on the whole this breed, now accustomed to the rather soft life on English farmland, gives relatively poor sport compared to their wilder cousins that flight off our winter coasts and estuaries.

A theory has been advanced that the Canada goose was not named as a result of its geographic origins, but that it came from *kanata*, an Iroquois Indian word, which incidentally had nothing to do with birds – let alone geese – and was purely the result of a misinterpretation by some early explorers. We shall probably never know.

Canada Goose and goslings at nest

M.J.PLEDGER

WOODCOCK

Scolopax rusticola

Plate XXIII

THE woodcock has always been a bird of mystery. Until its movements were monitored with radio-tracking devices comparatively little was known about its breeding habits; much still remains to be learned about other aspects of its life. It is widely distributed as a breeding species in temperate regions of Europe and Asia, as far east as Japan. In North America it is replaced by the smaller, but otherwise similar *Philohela minor*, nick-named the timber-doodle. Cock and hen woodcock cannot be told apart.

Although closely related to shore birds and officially classed as a "wader", as its name suggests the woodcock is found mainly in woodland. It is a solitary, retiring species, often going unnoticed due to its superbly camouflaged plumage, its silent flight and its nocturnal or crepuscular habits. Shakespeare referred to dusk as "cockshut" time.

In southern Britain its most favoured breeding habitat consists of dry, secluded, broad-leaved or mixed woodland, with frequent clearings and a light ground-cover of brambles and bracken with a carpet of fallen leaves. Skylights in the canopy for quick escape and easy access are essential. In northern Britain birch woods are frequented, and in many cases young forestry plantations are being increasingly utilised for breeding.

In winter woodcock will spend most of the daylight hours hiding or sleeping in cover – especially rhododendrons, holly or gorse – flying out at dusk to feed on pasture fields. Feeding will also take place in daylight if the night-time conditions do not allow a sufficient quantity of food to be ingested. At all seasons the diet is composed of earthworms and other soil-dwelling invertebrates, particularly insects and their larvae. Most of their food is obtained by probing in soft ground with the long bill. This has a prehensile tip which enables worms to be seized as with forceps. Large worms tend to be swallowed head first, sometimes after quite a struggle if the worm coils its body round the bird's bill. For a long while it was believed that food was located solely by touch, but recent research suggests that smell may be involved as well. Prolonged spells with frozen ground, as in the 1962–63 winter, cause heavy mortality amongst woodcock and – with migrating northern populations from Scandinavia and the Western Soviet Union augmenting the winter numbers in Britain – such hard weather can severely deplete breeding stocks in Britain and Europe.

Nobody yet knows how many of our winter woodcock are home bred and how many are migrants. The first noticeable falls of 'cock arrive on our shores from across the North Sea about the period of the November moon, which is traditionally called the "woodcock moon." For the sea-crossing the birds seem to prefer clear skies and light easterlies: there is some evidence that they fly at a considerable height.

The woodcock's breeding system is unusual in that males are almost certainly polygamous: one bird may mate with several different females during a season. Males do not defend an exclusive area to which females are attracted, and in which nesting takes place. The onset of breeding is characterised by the strange display flight termed "roding". From February to July, at dusk and dawn, the male travels in ghostly fashion above the woodland canopy at frequent intervals uttering a series of curious croaks, followed immediately by a far-carrying squeak. When the hen starts to lay, the male breaks off the relationship and abandons her.

The clutch of eggs – normally four – is laid in a small depression in the ground, lined with little else but dead leaves and invariably sited beneath a bramble stem or fallen branch. The female alone incubates, sitting motionless for long periods and relying on her camouflage for protection. They do, however, fall victims to foxes. The eggs hatch after 21 days and the young fly when 3 weeks old. Unusually for a wader, the young are fed by the parent for the first few days after hatching.

The woodcock is credited with the ability to carry her young away from danger or to better feeding areas; there are innumerable eye-witness accounts of this happening. The bird also has several other unique features, one being its enormous eyes which enable it to see sufficiently well to move around at low light intensities. Their positioning, high up on the head, also provides the bird with 360-degree vision, even with the bill immersed. The tiny pin feathers, (or vestigial first primaries), are highly prized by sportsmen and often worn in their hatbands. At one time they were used by artists and miniaturists.

The woodcock is one of the few birds to be traditionally cooked and eaten with the trail in place, i.e. without being first eviscerated. A generation or so ago a cold roast woodcock, accompanied by claret, was a much favoured breakfast for a country squire.

Woodcock with nest and eggs

M.J. PLEDGER

COMMON SNIPE
& JACK SNIPE

Capella gallinago/Lymnocryptes minimus

Plate XXIV

THREE species are likely to be of interest in European circles. The great or double snipe, which is a rare bird in our islands: the common, full or whole snipe, and the diminutive jack or half snipe – both of which are reasonably common. Their respective weights are approximately 8 oz, 4 oz and 2 oz. At one time the bird was called the "snite," a derivation of snout and a reference to its curious long bill. The French *bécassine* is similarly adapted from *bec* or beak, as is the German name.

This small, rather secretive wader is rarely found far from fresh water, preferring marshes, bogs, water meadows, wet moorlands and the soft edges of ponds, ditches, lakes and streams. It particularly favours places where the cover is patchy and tussocky, giving it shelter from wind at ground level. Here, where the ground is soft and damp it can probe for earthworms, cranefly larvae and other such food items.

It is a mistake to think that snipe like to wade about in water for any length of time. They frequently use the tussocks and cushions of grass for drying out and resting. They are especially fond of sewage farms and areas enriched with animal droppings. Productive Irish bogs were sometimes dressed with animal blood and waste from slaughter houses, and man-made Dutch snipe beds with manure and loads of decaying vegetation. In spite of this – perhaps because of it – snipe are succulent to eat!

Before swallowing an earthworm a snipe will, if possible, wash it carefully in water to remove any earth or grit that may be adhering. If it is foraging some distance from water it will often take the worm by the middle and suck it through compressed mandibles, so that the mud is left on the outside. A charming description of a tame snipe washing her worms in a pie-dish full of water appears in Longman's "Fur and Feather" series published at the turn of the century.

The small, but widespread resident population in the United Kingdom is supplemented in the winter months by an influx of migrants from Continental Europe, including numbers of jack snipe – a species which does not breed with us.

The common snipe has been nick-named the "heather bleater," because of the curious bleating or drumming sound emitted during the breeding season, when it undertakes its spectacular aerial display. This takes the form of diving down to earth with wings half closed and outer tail feathers quivering and vibrating like a reed instrument. During the last century the sporting journals were full of letters arguing as to how the noise was made – with the vocal chords or the tail feathers?

The drumming of snipe is a truly wild noise: evocative of isolated places and soft spring days.

Snipe will nest from May to August in tussocky cover, usually close to water or wetland, occasionally on dry moors. The clutch normally consists of 4 eggs: a variable olive-brown background, with one end blotched and speckled with sepia markings. After hatching the small brood is divided between the two parents, each half of the family feeding and roosting some distance apart to increase the chance of chick survival.

The adults fly with a dashing, zig-zag flight, starting up with a grating alarm call – usually rendered as "scaap" – which sounds like ripping calico. Due to this jinking flight and the probability that the gun is walking on uneven boggy ground, snipe can provide very difficult targets.

JACK SNIPE

This tiny little gamebird has a rather local distribution, but it should be possible to find it almost whever common snipe exist. Their habits are somewhat different. Whereas the common snipe flies up and away like lightning, the jack – rising slowly and silently – has a rather sluggish and a much shorter flight. Its sits tight until almost trodden on, and across the Channel was called the "deaf snipe" because it was so easily approached. Jack snipe are more solitary than the common species, and usually rise singly, rarely in wisps.

The food of the jack does not differ greatly from that of the common snipe and includes earthworms, small molluscs and insects. But it will accept more vegetable matter in hard weather, thus helping it – so said the old naturalists – to withstand poor feeding conditions.

It is sad to think that wetlands are for ever being drained to grow more food which is already in surplus in Common Market countries. And so, championed, mostly by the hunter, the snipe's habitat dwindles away.

Common Snipe wading – Jack Snipe on edge of marsh

"What is man without the beasts? If all the beasts were gone, man would die from great loneliness of spirit, for whatever happens to the beasts also happens to man. All things are connected."

Chief Seatlh
Suquamish Indian Tribe 1855

Select Bibliography

Bannerman, David A.	*The Birds of the British Isles (Oliver & Boyd, 1963)*	
Bent, A. C.	*American Gallinaceous Birds (Dover)*	
Coles, C. L. (Editor)	*Complete Book of Game Conservation*	*(Barrie & Jenkins, 1971)*
Coward, T. A.	*Birds of the British Isles*	*(Warne, 1929)*
Cramp Stanley (Editor)	*The Birds of the Western Palearctic Vol. 1*	*(Oxford University Press, 1980)*
Gladstone, Hugh S.	*Record Bags and Shooting Records*	*(Witherby, 1922)*
Johnson, Morris D.	*Feathers of the Prairie*	*(North Dakota Game and Fish Department)*
Leopold, Aldo	*Game Management*	*(Scribner, 1948)*
Lloyd, Llewellyn	*Gamebirds and Wildfowl of Sweden and Norway*	*(Day and Sons, 1867)*
Lovel, Dr T. W. I. (Editor)	*Woodland Grouse Symposium*	*(World Pheasant Association, 1978)*
Macpherson, H. A.	*The Pheasant – Fur, Feather and Fin Series*	*(Longmans, 1896)*
	The Grouse – Fur, Feather and Fin Series	*(Longmans, 1904)*
Ogilvie Grant, W. R.	*Handbook to the Game Birds*	*(W. H. Allen, 1897)*
Owen, Myrtyn	*Wildfowl of Europe*	*(Macmillan, 1977)*
Sharrock, J. T. R.	*The Atlas of Breeding Birds in Britain and Ireland*	*(British Trust for Ornithology and Irish Wildbird Conservancy, 1976)*
Starker, Leopold Dr A.	*The California Quail*	
Tegetmeier	*Tegetmeier on Pheasants*	*(The Field, 1904)*
Todd, Frank S.	*Waterfowl*	*(Harcourt Brace Jovanovich, 1979)*
Vandervell, C. A. and Coles, C. L.	*Game in the English Landscape*	*(Debrett, 1980)*
de Visme Shaw, L. N.	*Snipe and Woodcock*	*(Longmans, 1904)*
	Wildfowl	*(Longmans, 1905)*
Witherby, H. F. et al.	*The Handbook of British Birds*	*(Witherby, 1947)*
Game Conservancy Advisory Booklets		